Free Grace
Versus
Free Will

Free Grace Versus Free Will

W. E. Best

BAKER BOOK HOUSE
Grand Rapids, Michigan

Contents

Free Grace
Versus
Free Will

Introduction

"The lip of truth shall be established for ever. . ." reads Proverbs 12:19. Indeed, truth is truth, but truth can become adulterated. Of this we must beware. The man of God must never *wrest* the Scriptures or *handle them deceitfully* (II Peter 3:16; II Cor. 4:2). He must always remember that truth is based upon the sense of Scripture rather than its *sound*. Scripture must be compared with Scripture to discover the truth of any Biblical subject.

This especially applies to the ongoing discussion of free grace versus free will. John 6:37, which reads, "him that cometh to me I will in no wise cast out," *sounds* to many as though anyone can come to Christ. However, the *sense* of the verse is entirely different. The first part of the verse states, "All that the Father giveth me shall come to me. . . ." Hence, only those given to the Son by the Father *come* to Him.

The opposing positions on free grace versus free will, Calvinism and Arminianism, have their roots in the thought of Augustine and Pelagias, respectively. Augustine (354-430) revealed his stance on this issue in his *Confessions*. He believed that when Adam fell, all his posterity fell with him. "All men are depraved," said Augustine. He held that men do not have free wills, but are enslaved in sin. Pelagias (c. 360-420), on the other hand, denied the total depravity of man. He stressed that man has free will and can be saved whenever he so desires.

Like Augustine, John Calvin believed in free grace; and like Pelagias, Jacobus Arminius believed in the free will of man. There was no compatibility between the ideas of Augustine and Pelagias, and there was none between Calvin's views and those of Arminius. Furthermore, there is no intellectual harmony today between those who believe in free grace and those who believe in free will. The former hold that the sovereign God is on the throne and man is at His feet; the latter credit man with the authority to choose God or reject Him.

Advocates of free grace accept the Biblical doctrine of predestination. They also embrace these Biblical truths: (1) Man is a fallen creature and has no free will to do that which is spiritually good. (2) Justification is through faith, which is God's gift. (3) The gifts and calling of God are bestowed without repentance on God's part as well as the believer's.

Supporters of free will deny the Biblical doctrine of predestination and affirm the following: (1) The human race possesses a free will to do that which is good. (2) Justification comes by a faith which deserves salvation. (3) Since man's faith comes from himself, he has no assurance that he will not someday lose it. (Arminians are divided into two camps on this issue. Some believe a person may be saved today and lost tomorrow. Others believe that once a person is saved he is always saved.)

Now that the basic positions have been sketched, let us consider what the Scriptures say concerning free grace versus free will.

1

Freedom of the Will

EPHESIANS 1:11

The Biblical idea of freedom of the will can only be understood by studying it from the beginning of the Bible. But then, a study of any Biblical truth must begin in this manner. Just as the wrong stops pulled out on an organ bring disharmony, a few isolated Scripture verses taken out of context appear to teach things that do not harmonize with all the teaching of God's Word.

Absolute freedom of the will can belong only to God. No law restrains God's will, because He is His own law. Since God is sovereign, no power can overcome His will. He is omnipotent. He "... worketh all things after the counsel of his own will" (Eph. 1:11). God's will is irresistible, fixed, and everlasting: "... For who hath resisted his will?" (Rom. 9:19). It is everlasting because God does not change: "For I am the Lord, I change not ..." (Mal. 3:6). The Lord Jesus Christ, the second Person of the Godhead, is the same yesterday, today, and forever (Heb. 13:8). With God there "... is no variableness, neither shadow of turning" (James 1:17). God's will cannot be changed for the better because God cannot be better. It cannot be changed for the worse because God cannot be less than He is.

God's will is subject to no one, but the will of every man is subject to God. God did not determine to save men on the basis of their will to be saved. Had He so resolved, man's will would determine God's will. But that is impossible (and heretical)—God's freedom indicates that He is under no compulsion outside of Himself. He acts according to the law of His being. God is self-moved, and unable to sin.

The more intense the power of self-determination, the more intense the freedom. Consequently, *freedom of the will is attributable to God alone*. Every creature is responsible to Him. A will self-determined to absolute holiness—God's will— is marked by the highest freedom. Freedom in God is *immutable self-determination;* conversely, freedom in a finite being—Adam before the fall—is *mutable self-determination.* The truth that freedom in God is immutable self-determination is the key to the remainder of the discussion of the freedom of the will.

God's will is the law of the universe, not man's will. If there were no such being as the supreme, determining Jehovah, the universe would quickly become chaotic. If there were no free-electing love, every minister would close his lips, and every sinner would sit down in mute despair. Scripture records no instance of a limitation to God's will. His will of purpose is supreme, and it is accomplished without defeat (Rom. 9:19; James 1:17). But we need to distinguish between God's will of purpose and His will of command. Men are responsible to fulfill the latter, but God's will of purpose is not fully revealed to man: "The secret things belong unto the Lord our God: but those things which are revealed belong unto us and to our children for ever . . ." (Deut. 29:29).

But what about Adam's will and self-determination? Adam was created in a state of *uprightness*. Uprightness is a higher state than innocence: ". . . God hath made man upright; but they have sought out many inventions" (Eccles. 7:29). Some refer to Adam's uprightness as "original righteousness"; others call it "created righteousness"; and some label it "holiness." Adam's uprightness was righteousness and holiness in a sense, but it was not absolute. Adam's holiness, righteousness, or uprightness was *mutable*, because God cannot create God. Whatever God creates must be less than Himself.

Some believe that Adam was created in a state of equipoise, or indifference. He was inclined toward neither good nor evil. Hence, he could turn to either the Creator or the creature. Since he turned to the creature, he made the wrong choice. This erroneous view has been refuted by great scholars of the past. Scripture disproves the assertion that Adam was created in a state of indifference.

An actual state of indifference has never been found to exist; an uncommitted will has never occurred within human consciousness. In any event, it is unnecessary to assume absolute indifference to holiness and sin to account for Adam's fall.

Innocence does not sufficiently describe Adam's condition of uprightness. Original uprightness consisted of positive qualities. Adam's positive intellectual and moral qualities before the fall were manifested in his ability to name the animals (Gen. 2:20) and in his fellowship with the Creator (Gen. 2:15-25). Some knowledge of the animals' characteristics was necessary to name them. Furthermore, positive uprightness was necessary to enjoy positive fellowship with God.

The fact that God created Adam upright means that Adam had knowledge of God. This is explained as follows: The three faculties or powers in the human soul are (in this order) *understanding, affection,* and *will.* The order cannot be reversed. Eve's sin verifies the order of the powers of the soul. She gained *knowledge* of the forbidden fruit by seeing it. Her *affection* went out to the fruit of which she had gained knowledge. She then exercised her *will* by taking the fruit. Therefore, since Adam was created with an understanding of God, an uncommitted will was impossible. Consciousness always reports an inclined will, not an indifferent will. This is why Adam's uprightness was beyond mere innocence.

Uprightness includes several characteristics. Adam was created *upright*, an *adult*, a *spirit* and *with a will*. He did not come into the world as all others have. The first man was created mature, without the necessity for physical and mental growth and development. The idea that Adam had advancing stages in growth and learning contradicts the thought of created maturity. Adam's maturity proves that he had an *inclined* will. He was not in a state of equipoise, but his will was inclined toward God, his Creator.

In created maturity, Adam's intellectual faculties contained innate ideas and patterns. Therefore, his maturity enabled him to not only name the animals but commune with God. Adam was created a *spirit* (Gen. 2:7). The creation of a finite mind, or spirit, implies the creation of uprightness. *Spirit* must be distinguished from *matter*. Furniture is matter and must be moved by force. Adam was *self-determined* from within. His ability to move from within signifies his freedom. He was self-motivated and not moved by external force. Self-motion is self-determination, and self-determination is the act of the will.

Adam's will was a free will because it was self-determined. That which is not forced from without is free—but not absolutely. Adam was responsible to God. He was free in the sense that he was unconscious of any necessity imposed upon him. God's freedom is immutable, but Adam's freedom was mutable self-determination.

By the creative act, Adam's will was inclined to God—and that before it made any choice. He was created a spirit, and was self-determined the instant he was created. His self-determination was created with his will. Adam could not have been created uninclined. Adam's holy creation in original righteousness (or uprightness) was both created and self-determined. Viewed with reference to God, it was created. Viewed with reference to Adam, it was self-determining, self-ruling, and unforced from without.

Adam came into the world inclined toward God. That holy inclination was at once the *Creator's product* and the *creature's activity*. Adam did not find himself in a position to choose either the Creator or the creature as an ultimate end. He was inclined toward the Creator. His very uprightness was God-given, and did not proceed from his own ability. In fact, Adam's mutable self-determination led to his fall, and after the fall his will was enslaved to sin.

After his fall, Adam passed from inclination toward God to inclination toward sin. The radical change of his will cannot be accounted for by an antecedent choice from an indifferent state of the will. The radical change could not have occurred if Adam had been created in a state of equipoise. He fell from a state of mutable uprightness. To fall from a state of indifference would not have been such a tragic fall.

Since Adam's fall, the will of every person is inclined toward sin by nature. It remains so until the Spirit of God regenerates him. Then, his will is inclined toward God by grace. The work of regeneration in an individual produces as radical a change as the fall caused in Adam. A regenerated man has been created anew in Jesus Christ: "For we are his workmanship, created in Christ Jesus unto good works . . ." (Eph. 2:10). The new man ". . . is renewed in knowledge after the image of him that created him" (Col. 3:10). "And you hath he quickened, who were dead . . ." (Eph. 2:1). ". . . God . . . worketh in you both to will and to do of his good pleasure" (Phil. 2:13). God gives a new heart and a new spirit (Ezek. 36:25-27).

Adam's original uprightness was self-determined but not self-originated. His fall, however, was both self-determined and self-originated. The doctrine of concurrence—cooperation—cannot be connected with Adam's sin or his fall. God is the author of neither Adam's sin nor his fall.

The first existence of a virtue could not have come from man, for God is the original cause of all things. However, God uses second causes. Adam, the second cause, was created in a state of mutable self-determination, which allowed the possibility of his fall. And he did fall when he went from an inclination toward God to a selfish, ego-centered inclination. Sinful inclination is the *creature's* product and activity.

Mutable Adam, unlike his immutable Creator, could and did lose his uprightness. Adam was able to persevere in his holy self-determination, but he was able also to begin a sinful self-determination. His self-determination was to an ultimate end and not to a choice of means to an end.

Inclination differs from volition as the end differs from the means. Adam fell in his heart *before* he ate the forbidden fruit. Eve, the weaker vessel, was deceived but Adam was not. He was self-determined; that is, he desired to eat that he might be with his wife. The inclination preceded his choice. Eve also had sinned in her heart before she sinned externally.

It is not the committing of a sin that makes one a sinner. He is already a sinner before the act is committed. The Lord Jesus Christ identified sin as that which proceeds from the heart: ". . . whosoever looketh on a woman to lust after her hath committed adultery with her already in his heart" (Matt. 5:28). The desire that precedes the volition is sin.

Eating the forbidden fruit did not *originate* Adam's inclination, but it did *manifest* it. His will inclined to an end, and he chose the means to accomplish the end result. The will chooses because it is already inclined.

This is the reason there is no compatibility between the social gospel and the gospel presented in the Word of God. Those who proclaim a social gospel contend that men are not responsible for their acts of sin. They attribute sin to environmental or social conditions, which relieves sinners of their responsibility in committing sin. But this is nonsense. Sin cannot be attributed to another person or thing. Adam blamed Eve for his sin, and subtly put the blame on God Himself, who had given him Eve. But Adam's rationalization did not alter the facts. He had sinned responsibly. He had gone from inclination toward God to inclination to satisfy his own evil desire.

Adam's sinful determination originated within himself. God did not cooperate in Adam's evil self-determination. He created Adam a *free person*. Arminians maintain that a man cannot act freely unless he has the ability to cancel his act. This is not valid, however. If a man jumps from a building to commit suicide, even though he may change his mind on the way down, he cannot return to the top of the building. His self-determination is a free act, but he cannot reverse the act. In this same way, once Adam sinned he could not return to his original state. He fell—body, soul, and spirit.

The fall of man has been compared to the collapse of a dilapidated three-story building. Man's spirit may be compared with the top story, his soul with the second story, and his body with the basement. The first to be affected by the fall was his mind, or spirit. His emotions were influenced, and both intellect and emotions influenced his body. The top story fell into the second, and both fell into the basement. The whole man was affected in the fall. That is the reason people die physically (Rom. 5:12). Once Adam was self-determined to turn from God and satisfy his own desires, he could not return to his original righteous state.

A volition can change a volition, but it can never change an inclination. One choice can change another, but it cannot change the original desire. A person may choose to commit murder, and before pulling the trigger of the gun, change his mind. He has made a choice. His second choice has counteracted the first, but it did not erase the evil inclination of murder that was in his heart. The inclination can be removed only by God's grace. The power of God alone can overcome and do what man cannot do for himself.

So, therefore, the potential to reverse a sinful inclination is not necessary to make a person responsible for the inclination. The only thing necessary is that he originate it. Adam did originate his sinful self-inclination. He was not only the originator but was active in the origination. Before the fall, power to self-determine evil was unnecessary to Adam's self-determining holiness.

It is important to realize that Adam's understanding was unalterable, but his will was mutable. Certain facts, such as rudiments of arithmetic, cannot be unlearned. However, the will can be radically, totally changed. The fall of Adam's will was a revolution, not an evolution.

Let us summarize. In his fall, Adam did not choose between God and the creature. Adam's sin in the garden of Eden was not committed in a state of indifference, as though God was on his right and evil desire on his left. He was in a state of uprightness, inclined toward God, but by self-determination he turned from God to evil. That was not a choice between the Creator and the creature. He went from an inclination toward God to an inclination toward evil, and that was his fall.

Spontaneity in an animal is mere physical instinct, but spontaneity in a man is based on a capacity to reason and understand. He is a rational being and does not act from mere instinct. Inclination precedes man's act. Something appeals to his understanding, his affections are influenced, and his will acts accordingly. Arminians, on the other hand, assert that the will is both the determiner and the determined. That would indicate that the will is both cause and effect. But we have seen that the will is the last of the three ordered faculties of the soul. It does not cause an inclination. If the will causes understanding, we can as easily say that the tail wags the dog. If a person has a spiritual mind and has heard spiritual things, his affections are moved toward those things, and he acts accordingly.

After the fall, Adam's will was enslaved to sin and had lost its natural liberty. Let us state here that moral liberty is not essential to natural liberty. A man may choose his wife, profession, home, and so forth, but he does not have the power to choose that which is spiritual. It is not necessary for a man to have spiritual ability in order for his will to act naturally.

Man's acts of will are of two kinds: (1) Actions of the soul that are manifested in physical acts. One decides to do something and makes movement in that direction. Many follow an act of the soul when they walk the aisle, or stand before a church congregation asserting that they are following Jesus. (2) Actions of soul that occur within the soul itself. This happens when one wills to love God. It cannot be accomplished by the natural man who hates God (Rom. 3:8-18; John 3:19-21). If a person's desire to know the Lord is genuinely motivated by the Spirit of God, he does not seek the Lord in vain (Matt. 7:7). He who sincerely seeks the Lord gives evidence of the inworking of God's grace; we do well to remember that God does not begin anything He cannot bring to completion.

Since the fall, man by nature can do only evil. When a person is born again, however, he has the potential to do good. Although he is strongly inclined to good, he is still tempted and sometimes does evil. In a state of glory this will no longer be the case and man will be included only toward good.

2

Slavery of the Will

JOHN 5:40

There was a radical change in Adam's will in the fall, and he was enabled to return to God by another radical change. It was not Adam who sought God, but rather God who sought Adam. The enslaved will cannot of itself love God. Men who love God, then, do so because God first loved them (I John 4:10).

The enslaved will is controlled by its affections, which are evil, earthly, and sensual (James 3:15). As Adam's will acted according to his nature after the fall, so every sinner's will is free only to act according to his nature. The action of the will is determined by the nature of the person making the choice. The carnal mind is at enmity against God (Rom. 8:7). The grace of God alone can change the will that is enslaved to sin and cause it to become enslaved to Jesus Christ. True freedom is found only in this slavery: "For he that is called in the Lord, being a servant, is the Lord's freeman: likewise also he that is called, being free, is Christ's servant" (I Cor.

7:22). The Scriptural witness to freedom is limited to man's relation to God.

Man's enslavement signifies not impotence but rather sin, guilt, rebellion, and alienation from the omniscient One. Man's sin manifests not his freedom but his *slavery*. The first lesson a person must learn is that he has neither the will nor the power to save himself. God gives both in regeneration. The change of the will in regeneration is as radical as was the change in Adam's will when he fell. He enjoyed freedom prior to his fall; then his will became *enslaved*. No person since Adam has ever had a free will. Men are free agents, but they do not have free wills. A person who ascribes salvation to man's free will knows nothing of free grace.

One who adheres to the doctrine of the free will of man recently made the following statements: Unfortunately God has no power over the will of man; that is, God cannot save a person against his will, but at the same time, He is unwilling that any should perish. God has made it possible for all men to be saved, but the Bible indicates that salvation depends on man's willingness to be saved. It would be a kind of tyranny if God saved people against their wills. And because of man's free will, it is obvious by the very definition of things that man can deny the will of God and frustrate His benevolent plan.

The above statements are often made by people who believe in free will. They dishonor the sovereign God and exalt fallen man. The facts are that the will of every unsaved person is enslaved to sin. He is free to go in only one direction. Like a waterfall, he is free to go down. Sinners are free to act according to their depraved natures. Man has neither the will nor the ability to come to Christ: "No man can come to me, except the Father which hath sent me draw him . . ." (John 6:44). "And ye will not come to me, that ye might have life" (John 5:40).

Controversy has existed and continues to exist over the *nature*, *freedom*, and *power* of the will.

Those who believe the nature of man's will is such that he can be saved any time he so desires follow the teaching of

Pelagias. Arminians believe the will determines itself. They make the will sovereign, declaring it to be the determiner and the determined. Hence, their belief makes the will stand apart from the other faculties and places it first in the order of the powers of the human soul.

Semipelagianists believe that man's will is free but it needs some assistance from the Lord. One of the dogmas of Roman Catholics places them in this category concerning the nature of the will.

During the Reformation between the years 1545 and 1563, the hierarchy of the Roman Catholic Church met intermittently to formulate their dogma. Their fourth canon law stated, "If anyone sayeth, that man's free will, moved and excited by God, by assenting to God exciting and calling, no wise co-operates towards disposing and preparing itself for obtaining the grace of justification; that it cannot refuse its consent, if it would, but that, as sometimes inanimate, it does nothing whatever and is merely passive; let him be anathema." The purpose for the council's meetings was not only to define doctrine as they believed it but to condemn the Reformers.

The early Reformers taught that there were two faculties of the human soul—understanding and will. They truthfully stated that understanding is first the cognitive, or perceptive, ability of the mind, and the understanding is comprised not only of the intellect but also of the conscience of man. However, further study of the subject revealed that there were three faculties in the human soul—understanding, sensibility, and will. Later, theologians believed the three faculties were better expressed by referring to them as understanding, affection, and will. (Affection was inserted in the place of sensibility.) And so, we see that the soul is a trinity: Its intellect is the power of knowing; its affections are the power of feeling; and its will is the power of choosing. The will is influenced by what is heard and understood; the affections are affected by the understanding; and the will is influenced to volition.

Man's will cannot be determiner and determined, cause and effect, or sovereign and servant. That would place the will first in the order of the powers of the soul. To assert that the will stands apart from the other faculties of the soul is asserting that there is a man within a man who can reverse the man and fly against him to break him in pieces. The idea that the freedom of the will orders, determines, and influences itself to choose is contradictory. If the will is influenced, or determined, as Arminians claim, something must cause it to be influenced, or determined.

The will is a self-determining agent, but it is not both determiner and determined. How can the mind act first and, by its own act of choice, determine what motive shall be the reason for its choice? Eve's choosing and eating the forbidden fruit was influenced: Satan enticed her, by telling her she would be like the gods. Therefore, her intellect was influenced, her affection went to the forbidden thing, and she chose to take it. Her taking the fruit was an act of will, but her will was influenced.

Man has the power to discern, discriminate, and express himself. The intellect perceives what shall be done; the conscience instructs the mind in what should be done. Therefore, the understanding is the stationary faculty of the soul. It can be perverted through improper instruction, but it cannot be radically changed.

Adam retained his intellectual capacities after his fall, and continued making natural choices. Every sinner chooses natural things. Nevertheless, he cannot make spiritual choices because he is depraved, is an enemy of God, hates God, and his will is not inclined toward God. He hates the light and will not come to the light lest his deeds be reproved (John 3:19-21).

Every unsaved person is self-centered and hates anything that interferes with his concentration on self. He desires his own will, is unconcerned about the will of others, and despises God's will. His will remains in that condition until it is changed by the grace of God. The naturally hard heart must be removed by God and replaced with a new heart (Ezek. 36:26).

Although the Israelites were God's chosen people, they had to be brought to the end of themselves. God's providence caused them to go to Egypt and serve under taskmasters until they knew their helplessness. God gave them the desire for deliverance, and they cried to Him for it. God hears the cry of every person in whose heart He has wrought the work of grace, and gives the desire for deliverance from worldly things and a delight in spiritual things. No person desires salvation in vain, because God who gives the desire also satisfies.

The person who desires to hear the gospel and is attracted to the fact that God so loved him that He gave His Son to die in his place as Substitute has a work of grace already in his heart. The will, the last faculty of the soul, is determined by preceding things—understanding of the mind and affection of the heart.

After one has begun the Christian walk, his desire for the Lord and the things of the Lord never diminishes. Instead, zeal increases with growth in grace and knowledge. Assurance, stability, and hope are gained through knowing that God brings to fruition whatever He begins.

Controversy exists over the *freedom* of the will. Pelagians maintained that there is absolute freedom of the will. Semipelagians believed that God gives equal ability to all men, and that some use it to become Christians, and others use it to reject Jesus Christ.

The dictionary defines free will as the doctrine that human action expresses personal choice and is not determined by physical or divine forces.

Arminians define free will as a power in the human will by which a person may accept or reject salvation. Their belief that man's free will enables him to choose good or evil denies depravity. (The majority among religionists are classified with Arminians.)

Scripture, however, states that no one can resist God's will (Rom. 9:19). If a person outside of Jesus Christ has the capability in his will to accept or reject Jesus Christ, he has greater ability than a Christian does, for a Christian's will is subject to the will of God (Phil. 2:12-13).

Advocates of free grace properly distinguish *free agency* from *free will*. Man's will is *not* free. Because of his fall, man's will is naturally biased toward evil. It is always inclined toward that which dishonors God. Fallen man is free to act according to his depraved nature. He is free *from* righteousness and free *to* sin: "For when ye were the servants of sin, ye were free from righteousness" (Rom. 6:20). Even right and honorable things (from the standpoint of civic righteousness) are performed from selfish motives and not for God's glory. One must possess the grace of God to do anything for God's glory.

A *free agent* has the power to will and to act as his will dictates. Free agency is the power to decide according to one's character. Every person is a free agent because he is not forced from without, but he does not have a free will toward God. Every individual is bound from within and can act only according to his own depraved nature.

Free will assumes an ability *in the will itself* to choose good or evil. That cannot, of course, be true of a depraved will. A will that spontaneously and of itself chose holiness could not be called depraved. But no such will exists in any human being. No person can embrace Jesus Christ of his own volition. Human will is naturally depraved. An individual does what his will desires. He goes downhill like a car without a motor until God by His grace changes his course. One who exercises his will to accept Christ, then, has already been given a new, changed will in regeneration.

Man did not lose the faculties necessary to make him a responsible person in the fall. He did not lose his reason, conscience, or freedom of choice; but he did lose his *moral freedom*, the power to make spiritual choices. Man is not a free *moral* agent because he cannot choose between good and evil. He chooses only evil.

Adam's self-determination to evil began and ended with himself. God was not involved in it. Conversely, the radical change that occurs in regeneration is self-determination prompted by the Spirit of God. In regeneration, the hardness that prevents the will from acting in the direction of God is removed (Ezek. 36:25-27). Therefore, by the power of grace, the will that was once inclined to evil is now inclined to God. God's operation on the enslaved will is not forced from without. He makes the will tender and pliant from within. The Holy Spirit is the efficient cause, and the human spirit is the recipient of the Spirit's involvement in the will's inclination toward God.

Controversy exists over the *power* of the will. Arminians believe the will has the ability to order, determine, and influence itself to act in respect to good or evil. They believe that man cannot be free without that power. But they confuse man's willingness with his ability.

If one admits free will (in the sense that absolute determination of events is placed in the hands of men), he would acclaim man greater than God, making man's will primary and God's will secondary. But we know that God's will precedes man's will. It is dependent on the will of none. The Arminian makes a god out of his own will. Consequently, he must believe there are as many gods as there are free wills, which is a kind of polytheism.

There is no validity in the Arminian statement that God gave the same ability to all and some use it to accept Jesus Christ while others use it to reject Him. This confuses man's unwillingness to respond to Christ with his inability. However, the two must remain separate.

Augustine denied that fallen man has the ability of himself to come to God. He made some important statements concerning the human will: (1) Man's liberty before the fall was the potential to sin or not to sin. (2) Since the fall, man has liberty to sin but no ability to do good. (3) In heaven, man will have liberty to do good but not evil.

Augustine is correct in his denial that fallen man has the ability of himself to come to God. His distinctions concerning the human will are also correct. In contrast to Augustine, professing Christendom is far removed from the teaching of the Early Church. The further men get from the early apostolic teaching, the greater their apostasy. Augustine stated that man's liberty before the fall was the ability to sin or not to sin. This is the same as saying God gave man power to persevere or not to persevere. (Adam was a peccable person and did not persevere.) Augustine distinguishes between free agency and free will in his statement that since the fall man has the liberty to sin. As a free agent, man has the liberty to sin, but he does not have the ability to do good. As Augustine stated, man will have the liberty to do good in heaven.

Before the fall, Adam was a free agent. Man is a free agent now, and he will be a free agent in eternity. But he is fallen now and cannot cease from sin: "Having eyes full of adultery, and that cannot cease from sin . . ." (II Peter 2:14). Man in grace has conflict with sin (Rom. 7), but he may confess his sins and thereby be restored to fellowship with the Lord. The general course of man in grace is always up: ". . . the path of the just is as the shining light, that shineth more and more unto the perfect day" (Prov. 4:18). In heaven, man will have the liberty to do good, but he will be unable to do evil. Throughout eternity he will use his free agency to praise and honor the Lord.

The Reformers taught that free agency belongs to God, angels, saints in glory, fallen men, and Satan himself. The Puritans affirmed that man does not have the ability to change his moral state by an act of will.

The Reformers were correct in their assertion. God is a free agent, but He cannot do evil. He does as He pleases but can do nothing contrary to His nature. Choices can be made only according to one's nature. Therefore, man outside of Jesus Christ can make no positive spiritual choices. A person may improve his circumstances and environment, but without a change in nature, he can not improve his spiritual status. In fact, his end will be worse than his beginning (Matt. 12:43-45; II Peter 2:20-22).

Satan cannot recover lost blessing by an act of his own will; neither can man. No provision was made for Satan's recovery, and no provision is made for the recovery of fallen angels. Fallen angels are reserved in chains awaiting punishment (II Peter 2:4; Jude 6). When God elected some of the angels, He kept them from falling. He did not, however, prevent all mankind from falling in Adam. Some from among fallen mankind were chosen to be saved. Therefore, there is hope for the elect in Jesus Christ from among mankind, but there is no hope for the fallen angels.

Satan had the power of self-determination. He was not tempted from without as Eve was (or as Adam was tempted through Eve). There was nothing outside of Lucifer to tempt him. That is the reason his fall left him without hope.

The Puritans correctly stated that man does not have the ability to change his moral state by an act of will. Man must be a free agent to be accountable to God. However, one cannot attribute moral agency to man. *Free agency* is the power to decide according to one's character. *Free will* is the power to change one's character by volition or choice. Free agency belongs to every man, but the power to change one's character by the exercise of the will does not belong to mankind. Man is free to use his hand, but the hand is not free. It does only what the man commands it to do. It is a slave to his muscles. An unsaved person must act in harmony with his deceitful, wicked, depraved nature. He cannot act contrary to that which is commanded by his heart.

The same God who has ordained all events has ordained the free agency of man in the midst of the course of events He foreordained. The gospel is not forced on the elect against their wills (Ps. 110:3). Their wills are changed through regeneration, which makes them willing to accept the gospel.

3

Depravity of the Will

JAMES 1:14, 15

There is a proverbial statement that sin is a child which no one wants to claim. No person in his state of depravity wants to admit that the child is his own. Men are anxious to commit sin, but they are reluctant to acknowledge that they either conceived or gave birth to it.

The apostle James traced sin from its proper source to its final result (James 1:13-15). Temptation to sin is not from God, but from oneself. In every society, men have begun very early in life seeking to cast the burden of sin from themselves to another. Children go forth from the womb speaking lies (Ps. 58:3).

James pointed to the origin of man's sin when he said that every man is tempted when he is drawn away by *his own* lust. The apostle did not say that man is drawn away by God, circumstances, or Satan. The word *temptation* is used two ways in Scripture: (1) It signifies trial when it is ascribed to God. God tried Abraham's faith (Gen. 22:1-14). Because

Abraham's faith was supernatural, he was able to endure the test. (2) It indicates an endeavor by solicitation or other means to draw a person into sin (James 1:13-15). That temptation is not of God but from man's own heart.

Man is tempted when he is drawn away by his own *lust*. James was not only referring to sexual uncleanness here. He was speaking of the corruption that possesses all of the soul's respective faculties—understanding, affection, and will.

Some people have been mistaken in trying to determine causes of sin. Men have blamed God Himself for sin. God's decree is not a cause of sin. Proper distinction must be made between God's decree and the actual action that brought sin into being. God's decree has no causal influence on sinful action, since a decree as such does not operate to effect the thing decreed. God's purpose is one thing and his actual bringing into being that which He purposed is another. Sin entered the world by Adam's fall and not by God's creative hand.

Everything decreed does come to pass in time, but God's foreknowledge of an action does not necessitate the action. Whatever man does, good or bad, he does with as much willingness as though his will were really free. Foreknowledge of an action does not actively influence the action itself. God remains omniscient, and He knows every deed that every man will perform. Nevertheless, we must distinguish between God's foreknowledge of a thing and the activity of the foreknown thing.

Men have also blamed heavenly bodies for evil on earth. But the stars and planets imprint nothing upon men nor impel them to do evil. Astrology is a false science that professes to interpret the influence of heavenly bodies on earthly affairs. The so-called science of astrology is a direct attack on God. Intercourse between stars and a human soul is impossible because intercourse between animate and inanimate objects is impossible. (The sun, moon, and stars do influence things that have a nature common with themselves.)

Astrologers know nothing of God's grace. The Bible condemns them, classifying them with magicians and soothsayers

(Dan. 1:20; 2:2, 10, 27; 4:7; 5:7, 15). Isaiah called them stargazers and monthly prognosticators (Isa. 47:13), and he besought the people to save themselves from them.

Neither are providence, the times, people, and circumstances the causes of sin. They are only the *occasions* for sinning. Those are all indirect ways by which men charge God with their own sin. A man denies his responsibility for sin when he blames something or someone for his own sin. Christians refuse to attribute their sin to God. When God's providence placed Bathsheba before David's eyes, David did not charge God with his sin of adultery. The providence of God placed a boat at Jonah's disposal, but Jonah did not accuse God with his sin of fleeing on the boat and seeking to avoid fulfilling God's commission to him. The corruption of the times serves only as an occasion to bring forth the manifestation of the depraved wills of lost men.

Neither is the constitution and temper of man's body a cause of sin. Reaction to certain chemicals in a person's body does not cause him to sin. The body was made to serve, not to command. The cause of evil lies deeper than what is revealed in the act of sin itself. Many irregularities of the body actually stem from the heart, and not vice-versa: "The heart is deceitful above all things, and desperately wicked: who can know it?" (Jer. 17:9). All evil proceeds from the heart: "But those things which proceed out of the mouth come forth from the heart; and they defile the man. For out of the heart proceed evil thoughts, murders, adulteries, fornications, thefts, false witness, blasphemies: These are the things which defile a man . . ." (Matt. 15:18-20). The actual committing of acts of sin does not cause a person's guilt for those acts. Rather, the determination of man's will makes him an alcoholic, an adulterer, a thief, or a liar: "Having eyes full of adultery, and that cannot cease from sin; beguiling unstable souls: an heart they have exercised with covetous practices; cursed children" (II Peter 2:14). A person with eyes full of adultery is one who is wholly seized and occupied in mind, heart, and will by gazing with desire. The same is true with every kind of sin.

Nor can man justly charge Satan with his sin. Satan *is* the tempter, and he is held accountable for the temptation, but the one who yields to his temptation is not excused. One man might plan a robbery and secure another man to carry out his plans, but the second man is not relieved of guilt. He also is responsible for the crime. In the same way, individuals who yield to Satan's temptations are responsible for their yielding.

What, then, is the cause of sin? It is found in man's *depraved will.* Jacobus Arminius claimed that all unregenerate men have by their free wills the power to resist the Holy Spirit, reject the offered grace of God, condemn the counsel of God concerning themselves, reject the gospel of grace, and refuse to open their hearts to Him who knocks. This is heresy. A more recent Arminian, following Arminius's teaching, correctly stated that man is totally unable to save himself, but heretically asserted that man is able to exercise his reasoning faculties and freedom of will and choice.

The Arminian cries, "Free will!" as though the will alone had escaped the fall—as though Adam's sin had not affected that noble, virgin faculty. When a conservative Arminian and a liberal debate the subject of man's free will, the Arminian will assert that man has a free will, and the liberal will declare that he has a divine spark. However, free will and divine spark do not essentially differ. Both views are erroneous.

Man is depraved—enslaved to sin. If man has a free will to choose good or evil, why do men universally choose evil? The reason is that their depravity reaches even to their wills: ". . . ye will not come to me, that ye might have life" (John 5:40). Men love darkness because their deeds are evil. They hate the light and will not come to it because they do not want their deeds exposed (John 3:19-21).

According to Arminians, the sinner possesses free will only while he is a sinner. When one becomes a child of God, he is subject to the will of God. Arminians say that all men can believe, but the Bible teaches that they cannot believe unless they are Christ's sheep (John 10:25-27). Arminians assert that all men can come to Christ, but the Bible teaches "no man can come to me, except the Father which hath sent me draw him . . ." (John 6:44).

Arminians make the greater subordinate to the lesser, but the Bible proves that God is greater than men. Therefore, there is no compatibility between the philosophies of those who believe in free will and those who believe in free grace. All who have received the grace of the sovereign God follow the teaching of God's Word on free grace.

Depraved man is allured and deceived willingly, drawn away to sin by his own lust. He is baited from *his own lust:* ". . . the corruption that is in the world through lust" (II Peter 1:4). The world is only the object, not the cause of his sin. Lust signifies desire for and inclination toward unlawful things. The desire for unlawful pleasures is the vice of sensuality. The desire for unlawful riches is the foundation for fraud. The sin of ambition causes one to use corrupt methods. The desire for religion without Christ is the foundation of idolatry and superstition.

Satan knows that suggestion is impotent without lust. The flame is the devil's, but the wood for the fire is in man's being. Man has the power to will and do natural (worldly) things, but he does not have the power to do spiritual things. Like a harlot, lust draws its victim into its embrace and then conceives, or becomes pregnant. Every man is drawn away by his lust and enticed. When his lust conceives, it brings forth sin. When sin is finished, it brings forth death. The conception is produced by the union of lust and will. Prompting passes into purpose. Desire passes into determination.

Depraved man is worse than a puppet or a robot. A puppet is guided by the skillful hand of the puppeteer, but the unsaved man is guided by the depravity of his own enslaved will. Man is a free agent in that he is not forced from without; but he does not have free will because he is bound within. Man's faculty of will was affected in the fall. He is able to reason and understand natural things, but he is unable to understand spiritual things: "But the natural man receiveth not the things of the Spirit of God: for they are foolishness unto him: neither can he know them, because they are spiritually discerned" (I Cor. 2:14).

Man cannot determine his will toward good; the grace of God alone can determine that direction of man's will. A diseased will cannot provide a spiritual cure—the cure must come from outside of man. Like produces like; therefore, a depraved will produces a depraved will.

Advocates of free will believe that unless man is completely free, God commands him to do what he cannot. Man's sin must be considered at this point. God is not the cause of man's sin; nor is He the cause of man's fallen condition.

We all would agree that a person has the right to demand payment from a thief for the things stolen from his home—whether or not the thief can pay. In the same way, God has the right to demand uprightness from man who is incapable of performing it because of his own sin. God commanded the man with a withered hand to stretch it forth (Luke 6:6-10). Although Lazarus had been in the grave four days and was stinking, the Lord told him to come forth (John 11). Although man is impotent, he is nevertheless responsible. He is incapable of repenting and believing apart from grace, but God commands him to do both (Acts 17:30; 20:21). While man was without strength, Christ died for the ungodly (Rom. 5:6). The entire scheme of grace is built upon the fact that although all men are incapable they are responsible, and that Jesus Christ died for His own among them.

Freedom from coercion is one thing, but freedom from within is another. Fallen man is devoid of spiritual power, and spiritual death is written over every person. Like Nicodemus, man is shut up to the new birth (John 3:1-18); and like the leper, he is shut up to the will of God (Luke 5:12). The Bible holds man responsible, but it also strips fallen man of spiritual power. All boasting is thereby excluded, and all glory is accorded to the sovereign God (Rom. 3:26-28).

Man in his natural state is *unable* to be willing and *unwilling* to be able to come to Christ. His will is totally depraved, which is a result of his fallen condition. It must be made clear that natural ability and spiritual inability differ. A person's natural ability enables him to attend the place where the Word of God is proclaimed. Lydia's natural ability gave her power to go to the place where she heard Paul expound the word of God. However, it was an act of the sovereign God that opened her heart to understand the proclamation by Paul (Acts 16:13-14). An individual's natural ability makes him responsible for his sin, but his depravity renders him spiritually unable to come to Christ. The depravity of the will is due to sin, and sin is the cause of man's lust. There is no hope for anyone apart from the grace of God.

4

God Dethroned
by Free Will

JOHN 5:40; ACTS 18:27; I PETER 1:18-25

The heresy of free will dethrones God and enthrones man. Supporters of free will insist that God would be unjust and tyrannical to control the will of man. They see nothing egoistic or Satanic in attempting to fetter and direct the will of God. These natural-minded men suppose their own foolish wills cannot be gratified unless the all-wise God consents to relinquish His will. The doctrine of the free will of man tears the reins of government from the hands of the sovereign God. God's character is maligned by every person who believes in free will. Depraved natures make men unwilling to submit themselves to God's will. Their inability prevents their coming to Jesus Christ: "And ye will not come to me, that ye might have life" (John 5:40).

The Arminian theory is polytheistic in its concept of the first cause. It yields to the same temptation of Satan that Eve did in the garden of Eden: ". . . ye shall be as gods . . ." (Gen. 3:5). Free will is attractive to natural men because it appeals to their pride. It impresses upon them the fact that they have supernatural power which gives them self-determination toward God, righteousness, and holiness. It is blasphemous to think that a man has the ability within himself to control the will of God!

The Arminian concept leads men to believe they must first ascend to God before God descends to them. Ministers and others who follow this notion appeal to men to come to Christ, telling them that if they will come to Christ, Christ will come to them. This contradicts Scripture. The Lord sees the affliction of His people and descends to deliver them. The Israelites did not first ascend to God—the sovereign God descended to help His helpless, chosen people (Exod. 3:7-8). The Lord Jesus Christ left heaven and all its glory to come into the world to save those the Father gave Him in the covenant of redemption: "For the Son of man is come to seek and to save that which was lost" (Luke 19:10).

The Holy Spirit alone has the prerogative to command people to come to Jesus Christ. He gives them power to come by regeneration. A minister who commands his hearers to leave their seats and come forward, giving the impression that they may come to Jesus Christ by their faith, assumes the prerogative of the Holy Spirit. No person can usurp the official work of the Holy Spirit to effectually call people to salvation. Ministers can only proclaim the Word of God, pointing men to the Lamb of God (John 1:29). Man has no ability to call others from darkness to light.

The Arminian approach is erroneous. The sinner cannot first ascend to God before the Lord descends to help him. The two Old Testament truths of the order of the vessels of the tabernacle (Exod. 25—40) and the order of the offerings (Lev. 1—5) reveal to us that God takes the initiative. The ark of the covenant with its mercy seat represents the place where God is. God's description of the vessels began with Himself and descended with each of the vessels—the golden censor, candlestick, table of shewbread, laver, and finally, the altar of brass where He met the sinner. The burnt offering, which represents what Jesus Christ is to God, was the first in order. The meal offering, showing what He is in His impecca-ble human nature, followed; then the peace offering, the sin offering, and the trespass offering, where God meets the sinner. This divine order is reversed by every person who believes in free will.

Arminians believe that man's will precedes God's will. However, God's will not only planned and provided salvation but applies it as well. God's application of salvation is opposed by the free will of Arminians—self-will is the essence of anti-Christian religions. Their supposition that God is tyrannical to save a person against his will is a misunderstand-ing of salvation. God works in a person to make him willing when He imparts regeneration: "Thy people shall be willing in the day of thy power . . ." (Ps. 110:3).

Arminians assert that free will belongs as much to man as it does to God. However, God's will alone is absolutely free. Once a person grants that the Creator is subordinated to the creature, he has joined forces with all the vain philosophies of the world. Man's religion places man on the throne and sub-ordinates God. God does not live for mankind—before God created man or any creature, He lived for *Himself*, and He continues to do so. God is immutable, and He will live for Himself forever: "For of him, and through him, and to him, are all things: to whom be glory for ever . . ." (Rom. 11:36).

The Arminian theory is contrary to Scripture because it denies depravity, indicating that the will of the sinner can, apart from grace, make a spiritual choice and has within itself power to turn from evil. Arminians insist that if an unsaved person was against Christ, he could not come to Christ, and since he can come to Christ, he is not against Christ. But Scripture says that the depraved will *is* against the Lord Jesus Christ: "He that is not with me is against me . . ." (Matt. 12:30). Notice that Christ did not say, "He that is not with me *is not* against me," but, "He that is not with me *is* against me."

Either Satan or the Lord Jesus Christ dominates every indi-vidual under heaven. Every *unsaved* person is dominated by Satan. He walks according to the course of this world, according to the prince of the power of the air. He is by nature a child of wrath (Eph. 2:1-3). The children of God, on the other hand, are dominated by the Lord Jesus Christ. They have been delivered from bondage to Satan and are made bondslaves of Jesus Christ (I Cor. 7:22-23).

Arminianism is opposed to the doctrine of divine election. Its followers think their doctrine of free will destroys that Biblical truth. But let the so-called free will do all it can—it cannot avoid sin and secure pardon if God withholds the Spirit of regeneration. If free will is the same in all men, why does it attain to salvation in some and not in all? Arminians cannot answer that question. The answer is found in free grace. "... As many as were ordained to eternal life believed" (Acts 13:48). The grace of God is what makes believers react differently from nonbelievers.

The Arminian theory rejects the Biblical doctrine of reprobation. However, Scripture teaches that God negatively and positively reprobates men for their own sinful condition.

There are at least seven truths that Arminians either do not know or willfully reject in the face of Biblical data:

First: Arminians reject the fact that the unrenewed will is set against the truth of God. The unrenewed will of man cannot understand spiritual things (I Cor. 2:14). He hates divine truth (John 3:19-21). He does not seek the Lord (Rom. 3:11). Conclusively, man's understanding, affection, and will are depraved. Since his understanding does not comprehend spiritual things, he has no affection for the things of God, and his will cannot be determined for the things of God.

Since desire for truth must be given by the Lord, truth is always offensive to the unregenerate. Natural men love darkness rather than light because their souls with all their faculties are depraved (John 3:19-20). They hate everything pertaining to righteousness, truth, and God because their deeds are evil. Persuasion by any means cannot draw a person to Christ. An individual cannot conjure within himself a desire to remedy his condition. He is unable to be willing. He must be drawn by a power outside of himself.

Second: Arminians reject the fact that the unrenewed will must be wrought upon by divine power. If the will of an unregenerate man were never wrought upon other than by moral persuasion, it would never be subject to the gospel of Jesus Christ. Natural man *does* have the light with which he was born: "That was the true Light, which lighteth every man that cometh into the world" (John 1:9). He is capable of weighing certain issues. He has a conscience that either accuses or excuses him: ". . . do by nature the things contained in the law, these, having not the law, are a law unto themselves: Which shew the work of the law written in their hearts, their conscience also bearing witness, and their thoughts the mean while accusing or else excusing one another" (Rom. 2:14-15).

Conscience must be *purified* by the blood of Jesus Christ to be void of offense (Heb. 9:12-14). Every person has within himself enough intuitive knowledge to render him inexcusable before God. He has the capacity to recognize the evidences that testify of the Creator's existence (Rom. 1:19-20). But natural man can have no spiritual light until the sovereign God in His good pleasure gives it. The Light of life (John 8:12) is possessed only by those who have been regenerated by the Spirit of God (Rom. 8:1-4).

Third: Arminians reject the fact that the natural impotence of the will cannot be cured by moral suasion. That is the general attitude among professing Christendom; therefore, Arminians adopt different tactics and gimmicks to attract people to their places of worship. Most of them will tolerate some doctrine, as long as they can have a part somewhere in the operation of the church program. They consider doctrine secondary because they feel they are reaching people with their programs. However, regeneration by the Spirit of God alone persuades men for Christ (I Peter 1:20-21).

Fourth: Arminians reject the fact that the unrenewed will of man does not spurn truth simply because he does not understand it. Some argue that the sinner will receive the gospel if it is made plain to him. That is the reason men have compiled so many versions of the Bible recently. But if explanation alone could convince men for Christ, they would love truth and reject error—and this is not the case.

Anyone who has been born again by the Spirit of God can understand the Bible, but apart from the new birth, he cannot understand God's Word regardless of its interpretation by man. A Christian has the mind of God, and has been enlightened by the Holy Spirit. His affections are moved by what he hears with his enlightened mind. His will is inclined and self-determined to embrace that which his understanding has received and his affection loves and desires.

The apostle Paul knew that unless the Spirit of God enlightened the minds of those who listened, they could not understand, regardless of the manner in which the Word was proclaimed. That is why the apostle never requested prayer that the gospel be simply stated or explained in a manner that could be understood by unsaved people. He only asked prayer that he might have freedom of the Spirit to proclaim the Word (II Thess. 3:1).

Arminian philosophy concerning simplification of the Word for man's benefit is a denial of the truth that man is depraved. Man's unrenewed will is set against the truth of God. The more clearly truth is set before him and pressed upon him, the more his hatred swells and rises. That reaction among men was demonstrated in response to the words of the Lord Jesus Christ Himself (John 6:41, 52, 60, 66). They "strove among themselves" (v. 52), and said the Lord's words were "an hard saying" (v. 60), and "walked no more with him" (v. 66). The Lord's words were filled with compassion, Spirit, and truth. A preacher has never been greater than He. Nevertheless, those hearers were unpersuaded. Conversely, all who have been regenerated by the Spirit of God respond to the word of God in the same way that Peter, the spokesman for the twelve, did when questioned by the Lord: ". . . Will ye also go away? Then Simon Peter answered him, Lord, to whom shall we go? thou hast the words of eternal life. And we believe and are sure that thou art that Christ, the Son of the living God" (John 6:67-69). That is the answer given by every person who believes the doctrines of grace.

Fifth: Arminians reject the fact that man's inability to fulfill the law does not arise from the nature of the law but from the corruption of man's will. Unregenerated man, however, cannot possibly fulfill the law of God. He cannot love the Lord with all his heart, soul, mind, and strength and his neighbor as himself (Luke 10:27). He can never love the Lord until he has first been loved by the Lord. Love is reciprocal: "Herein is love, not that we loved God, but that he loved us, and sent his Son to be the propitiation for our sins" (I John 4:10). Nevertheless, God can command man to do that which by his own sinful condition he is incapable of doing (Acts 17:30).

Sixth: Arminians reject the fact that man's unrenewed will is enslaved to sin and self. But Scripture teaches that man's will is enslaved to self and therefore it is enslaved to sin. A wealthy farmer demonstrated this truth in Luke 12:18-19. He did not have enough room to store his fruits and demonstrated his selfish will by saying, ". . . This will I do: I will pull down my barns, and build greater; and there will I bestow all my fruits and my goods. And I will say to my soul. . . ." Four times he referred to his own will. God's will did not enter his thoughts.

The majority among professing Christians will not tolerate the teaching that man's will is depraved because they do not want to believe that their own wills are depraved. They prefer hypocritical happiness and nondisturbance. But it is nonetheless true that unregenerated man's will is spiritually dead. It is only made active by the work of God in regeneration.

John 1:12 is often used to support the theory of free will. However, its context proves the contrary. The words "as many . . ." imply an antithesis. One cannot prove the doctrine of free will from these verses in the first chapter of John. The power, privilege, or right to become the sons of God is not potential but *actual.* The privilege does not indicate any sort of halfway faculty—the privilege is full and complete. The power is given to those who have already believed.

Arminians confuse the undefined potential with the present result. Men become *children* of God by regeneration, and they become *sons* of God by adoption. Those who believe have already been regenerated. Faith flows from its source—regeneration—and not conversely. When the Lord breathes faith into an individual, He regenerates him in a hidden and secret way unknown to that person.

Seventh: Arminians reject the fact that man's willing and running are the fruits of grace and grace is not the fruit of willing and running. But the ideas of free grace and free will are diametrically opposed. All who are strict advocates for free will are strangers to the grace of the sovereign God. Willing and running are *fruits* of grace: "So then it is not of him that willeth, nor of him that runneth, but of God that sheweth mercy" (Rom. 9:16). Men do not work and strive to get a ticket to heaven. That was furnished for the elect in the redemptive work of Jesus Christ. As a recipient of Christ's redemptive work, one lives and works for Christ. A believer is willing to die to self daily (I Cor. 15:31).

Contrary to Arminian teaching that man has the *will* to believe, Scripture affirms that he believes *through grace:* ". . . the brethren wrote, exhorting the disciples to receive him [Apollos]: who, when he was come, helped them much which had believed through grace" (Acts 18:27). Some affirm that the word *grace* in that verse applies to the gospel, and others think it refers to Apollos' eloquence. Neither of those interpretations will stand the test of Scripture. The God of nature is also the God of grace. His influence in the one dimension strikingly corresponds with His agency in the other. God not only brings creatures into the world of nature, but also provides for their support.

Genuine salvation consists of more than mental assent of the mind to certain truths: "For with the heart man believeth unto righteousness; and with the mouth confession is made unto salvation" (Rom. 10:10). A person first believes with his heart; then he confesses that salvation with his mouth. The state of his heart corresponds with his mind.

A peril of deception arises from the near resemblance between counterfeit and genuine faith. In time a person proves whether he has given mere mental assent to historical truths or has been regenerated by free grace. The individual in whose heart the Lord has worked a work of grace desires the Word of God that he might grow thereby (I Peter 2:2). Good works follow purification of the heart by faith (Acts 15:9; James 2:17-26). Faith works by love (Gal. 5:6).

Ungodly people give credit to the Scriptures in general but hinder the truth of God in unrighteousness (Rom. 1:18). Men have a tendency to be satisfied with a mere assent of the mind, which is void without obedience from the heart and change from glory to glory (Rom. 6:17; II Cor. 3:18).

Saving faith is through grace (Eph. 2:8-10). From the source of grace, the Object of faith comes as a revelation. The Lord Jesus Christ, the Incarnate Word, is the Object of faith. The Written Word which reveals the Incarnate Word is also an object of faith.

Saving faith is brought into existence by *divine production*. Christ Himself ascribed its origin to God the Father: ". . . flesh and blood hath not revealed it unto thee, but my Father which is in heaven" (Matt. 16:17). The exercise of faith comes from that divine source. It is then exerted in every condition of one's existence. It is manifested during prosperity, adversity, health, and illness, and in devotion and service. Since that God-given faith is maintained by Christ's intercession, it cannot be lost. The Lord Jesus Christ prayed for Peter that his faith fail not (Luke 22:32). The intercessory work of Jesus Christ guarantees the maintenance of one's faith.

No person can believe on the Lord Jesus Christ without the aid of God's grace (I Peter 1:18-21). He must first be regenerated by the Spirit of God. Believers are not passive recipients of God's grace. Their God-given faith has a purifying effect on their lives.

The believer in Jesus Christ needs constant assistance during his earthly pilgrimage. A person may question the reality of his faith, but Christians never deny the efficacy of divine, supernatural faith. Since faith comes from the grace of God, men are mistaken to think man has virtue, ability, or power to exercise his own free will and choice. Christians are what they are by the grace of God (I Cor. 15:10).

The grace of God leads its recipients to feel their deficiencies in knowledge, sanctification, and competence. They know nothing as they ought (I Cor. 8:2), but God has supplied assistance for every one of His children. He ordained the church with her divinely appointed elders to instruct and guide them that they might not be tossed to and fro (Eph. 4:11-16).

5

Predestination and Free Agency

ROMANS 8:29-30; EPHESIANS 1:5, 11

How can a person be a free and responsible agent if his actions were foreordained from eternity? *Free* and *responsible agent* indicates that an intelligent person acts with rational self-determination. The term *foreordination* signifies that from eternity God made certain the course of events that occur in the life of every person and in the course of nature. The same God who ordained all events ordained the free agency of man in the midst of those foreordained events. Free agency is under God's absolute sovereignty.

The gospel is forced upon none against his will. Man is made willing in the day of God's power (Ps. 110:3). If the absolute determination of events is within man's hands, man has become superior to God. His will has become primary and God's will, secondary. Conversely, the Bible teaches that God's will is supreme and does not depend on man. The will of God makes the will of man willing to embrace the gospel to which by nature he is opposed.

The word *predestination* is a translation of the Greek word *proorizo* which is made up of two Greek words. The suffix *horizo* means to mark out, appoint, decree, determine, or ordain. The prefix *pro* means fore, in front of, prior to, or before. Hence, the compound word translated *predestination* means to determine or appoint beforehand. This places limitation upon someone beforehand, and brings a person within the sphere of a certain future, or destiny. Conclusively, the foreknown have had limitations placed around them which bring them within the sphere of becoming God's children (Eph. 1:5) and of being conformed to the image of Jesus Christ (Rom. 8:29). Hence, glory and honor must be attributed to the sovereign God by every recipient of grace.

Only a person governed by natural feelings rather than a revelation of truth through a sanctified mind could accuse those who believe in absolute predestination of fatalism. One person erroneously said that the logical conclusion of believing that events occur as predetermined is that God is guilty of all manner of sin.

Others regard divine sovereignty and human responsibility as one of many Bible antinomies. They illustrate their belief by comparing the so-called antinomy to two natural forces— centrifugal and centripetal force. They say these are complementary forces which contribute to the harmonious operation of the universe, and are analogous to divine sovereignty and human responsibility. They conclude that antinomies in nature prove that there are antinomies in Biblical theology. They believe that since the Author of nature is the Author of revelation, one may reasonably conclude that Scripture contains difficulties analogous to those in nature.

However, the Reformers and Early Church Fathers correctly interpreted predestination and the free agency of man. They stated that the two Biblical truths do not conflict. The blending of the absolute sovereignty of God and the free agency of man is illustrated in every earthly kingdom. The king has the right to impose laws, and his subjects have the duty to observe them. God's right to impose law arises from his sovereignty. Man's duty to observe His law grows from his responsibility as a created being to his Creator.

Let us discuss *predestination* and *free agency* from three premises: (1) Biblical predestination is not fatalism. (2) Biblical predestination does not eliminate man's free agency. (3) Biblical predestination does not reduce the will of man to a mere machine.

1. *Biblical predestination is not fatalism.* The Mohammedan concept of predestination is fatalistic. In genuine fatalism, fate is a natural force. The fatalist excludes mind and purpose, and confuses God with natural law. According to the Stoic, God is natural law and His other name is Destiny. He believes that human actions spring from irrational forces. The Christian, however, is assured that actions proceed from the loving, heavenly Father. He can say with the psalmist, "The Lord is my shepherd. . . . He maketh me to lie down in green pastures: he leadeth me beside the still waters. He restoreth my soul: he leadeth me in the paths of righteousness. . . . Thou art with me; thy rod and thy staff they comfort me. Thou preparest a table before me . . . thou anointest my head with oil . . ." (Ps. 23).

If a fatalist were truly consistent, he would stop eating. After all, he is going to die anyway. And if it is his fate to live many years, he need not eat—he cannot die if his fate is to live many years. So, you see, no person can be consistently fatalistic. Since God has foreordained that a man shall live, He has also foreordained that he shall be kept from the suicidal folly of refusing to eat.

Fatalism is a heathen doctrine, but predestination is a Christian doctrine. It is called *destination* because it comprehends a determined order of the means to the end. It is called *pre*-destination because God appointed that order in and with Himself before the actual existence of those things He so ordered. God's providence completes in time what He predestined in eternity.

Predestination recognizes the order of the universe. Since God is the God of order, predestination not only calls attention to God but to theodicy—vindication of God in all His actions. Providence is predestination in execution, and predestination is providence in its intention. The Christian looks *through* and not *at* providence to behold the fulfillment of God's predetermined will. Therefore, he does not panic under circumstances but sees God's determination before the foundation of the world revealed through His providential actions.

The Christian is not in the hands of a cold, immutable determinism, but in the hands of the warm, loving, heavenly Father. The tribulation he experiences teaches him to give glory to God (Rom. 5:3-5). Every Christian's faith is so tested. Abraham's faith was severely tested when God told him to offer Isaac. Nevertheless, he willingly denied his own selfish ambitions and did as God commanded. The Lord prevented Abraham from slaying his son, and He provided a substitute (Gen. 22:1-13). Abraham was not actually required to slay his son, but the desire to fulfill God's will was in his heart. He looked through that providential act and saw the working out of God's eternal purpose.

Predestination signifies that God created all things, and His providence extends to all His works. God Himself is free, and He has provided that man shall be free within the limits of his nature. Although man does not have a free will, he is a free agent.

The certain salvation of some is no hindrance to the endeavors of all. Suppose a minister could assure an assembly of unsaved people that ten of them would be saved, but no one knew who the ten were. That would not discourage others in the congregation, and it would not discourage the proclamation of the gospel. It would cause everyone to want to be under the sound of the gospel because God calls by the gospel. Ministers who believe the truth of predestination may preach with conviction, determination, and assurance. The Word which is preached in all its purity will not return void but accomplish the purpose for which God sends it: "So shall my word be that goeth forth out of my mouth: it shall not return unto me void, but it shall accomplish that which I please, and it shall prosper in the thing whereto I sent it" (Isa. 55:11). Hence, persons who proclaim the truth become

". . . a sweet savour of Christ, in them that are saved, and in them that perish: To the one we are the savour of death unto death; and to the other the savour of life unto life . . ." (II Cor. 2:15-16). Divine predestination *assures* salvation to *some.* However, the Arminian assumption that Jesus Christ provided salvation for all makes it *sure* to *none*—every man must exercise his own free will, and there is no assurance that any will do so.

The primary reason a man is likely to object to predestination is his unwillingness to acknowledge that he is at the disposal of another. Man desires self-disposal rather than control by the sovereign God. An often-sung hymn that states that one was "a wandering sheep and *would* not be controlled" should be corrected to state that he would not *admit* that he was controlled. The truth of predestination destroys a person's pride and casts him at the feet of the sovereign God.

2. *Biblical predestination does not eliminate man's free agency.* God ordained human history and free agency in the midst of it. Self-determination belongs only to man. God has the right to make laws, and man is obligated to obey them. Man is responsible for his volition—his disposition, or inclination, is self-moved. An animal is not responsible for his volition because instinct is not self-moved. Spontaneity in man is rational self-determination, whereas in an animal it is nothing more than physical instinct. Man's spontaneity is the object of either approbation or disapprobation—his sense of reason makes him responsible. However, spontaneity in an animal is the object of neither approbation nor disapprobation. An animal is not a free agent.

Man's free actions are not excluded from God's foreordination. Moreover, God's foreordination should not be regarded as overriding man's free agency. Servitude of the depraved will does not turn history into a frivolous marionette show. Because Judas followed his own depraved desires, the Lord told him that it would have been good had he not been born (Mark 14:21).

The question concerning sin and holiness relates to *inclination* rather than to *volition.* Inclinations are born in man but choices are not; the will is not determined by the preceding state of mind. Consequently, a man is free so long as his volitions are conscious expressions of his own mind, or his activity is determined and controlled by his reason and fears.

Foreknowledge and foreordination stand or fall together. Since God knows even the most infinitesimal things (Matt. 10:29-30), it is contradictory to say He foreknows the certainty of an event which in its very nature is uncertain. Divine certainty does not conflict with free agency, since God's decree does not produce an event. The same decree that determines the certainty of an event also determines the freedom of the agent of the event.

If God's foreknowledge were inconsistent with free agency, His foreordination would be inconsistent with it. God is a free Agent, and it is a certainty that He will always do right. It is also a certainty that fallen men, Satan, and demons will always do wrong. The will of man does nothing by constraint from *without*, since outward determination of an act renders it not free. The will of man is, instead, constrained from *within*. Inward, rational determination demonstrates the freedom of an act. Action prompted from within proves the free agency of man. Although a person may be unaware of it, from the first to the last moments of his life, he acts in absolute subservience to the purposes and decrees of God concerning him.

3. *Biblical predestination does not reduce the will of man to a mere machine.* The alternatives to predestination are determinism and indeterminism. *Atheistic determinism* refuses to acknowledge God as the first cause. It goes no further with causes than the boundaries of this world. *Nonatheistic determinism* traces causality to God, but that kind of causality excludes human responsibility. Although the term *determinism* does come within the vocabulary of Christian conversation, the Christian doctrine of predestination and free agency presents something other than determinism and indeterminism. The word of God reveals the

almighty activity of God and human responsibility at the same time.

Determinism and free agency are incompatible. Hence, divine determinism differs from determinism as it is generally understood. The rigidity of determinism is found nowhere in the Scriptures, but neither are responsibility, guilt, and punishment crowded out by God's sovereign power. Every man "... shall give account to him that is ready to judge the quick and the dead" (I Peter 4:5). "So then every one of us shall give account of himself to God" (Rom. 14:12).

Those who believe that God's absolute sovereignty and man's responsibility are contradictory must embrace one of two erroneous perspectives. They make man the creator of events, and place history in his hands, or they make history a divine game in which human beings, void of responsibility, are pushed about like checkers.

A biblical understanding of God's sovereignty and man's free agency does not lead a person to be unconcerned about everything because all is predetermined. Many react in that manner after first coming to the knowledge of God's absolute sovereignty, but further instruction in the Word of God leads them to see man's duty. Predestination and responsibility are not competitive or mutually exclusive ideas as determinism would rationalize. The Bible teaches a divine activity *over* and *in* the activities of man. God overrules what He does not causally produce.